Penguin English
Introducing Linguistics

David Crystal is Honorary Professor of Linguistics
at the University College of North Wales, Bangor,
and formerly Professor of Linguistic Science at the
University of Reading. He is the author of several
Penguin books, including *Linguistics* and *Listen to
Your Child*, as well as of the *Cambridge Encyclopedia
of Language*. In the field of terminology he has
recently completed the third edition of his *Dictionary
of Linguistics and Phonetics* and a guide to linguistic
terms for the National Curriculum, *Language A to Z*.

Introducing

LINGUISTICS

David Crystal

PENGUIN ENGLISH

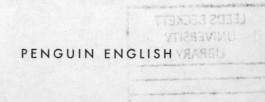

PENGUIN ENGLISH

Published by the Penguin Group
Penguin Books Ltd, 27 Wrights Lane, London W8 5TZ, England
Penguin Books USA Inc., 375 Hudson Street, New York, New York 10014, USA
Penguin Books Australia Ltd, Ringwood, Victoria, Australia
Penguin Books Canada Ltd, 10 Alcorn Avenue, Toronto, Ontario, Canada M4V 3B2
Penguin Books (NZ) Ltd, 182–190 Wairau Road, Auckland 10, New Zealand

Penguin Books Ltd, Registered Offices: Harmondsworth, Middlesex, England

First published 1992
3 5 7 9 10 8 6 4 2

Printed in England by Clays Ltd, St Ives plc
Set in 10/13 pt Lasercomp Times Roman

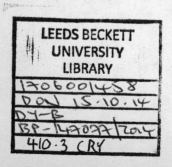

Introduction to the series

The aim of this series is to meet a need which has often been expressed by students encountering linguistics for the first time – to have a brief, clear and convenient guide to central concepts in the various branches of the subject, which would help them develop painlessly a sense of its range and depth. The idea is to provide a comprehensive outline of an area, which can be used as a general backup for lectures, a supplementary index for textbooks, and an opportune aid for revision. The information is organized alphabetically, for convenience of look-up, but it is presented discursively, with copious cross-references. The result is a somewhat unconventional kind of reference book – half-dictionary, half-encyclopedia – but one which offers considerable gains in accessibility and comprehension. The order of headwords is based on word-by-word alphabetization.

We have chosen topics for the first books in the series which are widely taught in introductory undergraduate and postgraduate courses. Along with linguistics itself, we have dealt with phonetics, English grammar, sociolinguistics, and psycholinguistics. Each has been written by an acknowledged leader in the field, in consultation with the general editor, and the result is a series which I believe conveys with authority, clarity, currency and consistency the core elements of this fascinating subject.

David Crystal

absolute universals see **universal**

acceptability The extent to which linguistic data are judged by native-speakers to be possible or normal in their language. Because of variations in regional and social background, age, sex, personal preferences, and so on, people often disagree as to whether an **utterance** is acceptable. For example, people brought up in a strongly **prescriptive** tradition of language teaching would view such sentences as *I will go* (for *I shall go*) and *She wants to immediately resign* (for ... *resign immediately*) as unacceptable. An acceptability test is an experiment in which native-speakers are asked to evaluate sets of utterances containing those language features over whose acceptability there is some doubt. An utterance considered unacceptable is marked by an asterisk; if it is marginally acceptable, it is given a question mark: *Each other couldn't be seen*; *?It was hoped to see them*. (See also **grammaticality**.)

acceptability test see **acceptability**

acoustic phonetics see **phonetics**

acquisition The process or result of learning a particular aspect of a language, and ultimately the language as a whole. The term is used both in relation to first language learning (often called **child language acquisition**) and the learning of a second or foreign language, though in both contexts a narrower definition can be found, in which it contrasts with a related notion. In foreign language learning, for example, acquisition (viewed as a subconscious natural process) is sometimes distinguished from learning (viewed as a conscious process which monitors the progress of acquisition). In generative linguistics, the **language acquisition device (LAD)** is a model of language learning in which the infant is credited with an innate predisposition to acquire linguistic structure.

actualization see **realization**

adequacy A level of success in the writing of grammars. The concept was introduced when the idea of a generative grammar was first being expounded. Three levels of achievement were postulated. **Observational adequacy** is achieved when a grammar generates all of a particular sample (or **corpus**) of data, correctly predicting which sentences are well formed. **Descriptive adequacy** is achieved when the grammar goes beyond this, and describes the intuitions (or competence) of the language's speakers. **Explanatory adequacy** is achieved when a principled basis is established for deciding between a series of descriptively adequate grammars. In addition, a grammar is said to be **weakly adequate** if it generates a desired set of sentences; it is **strongly adequate** if it does not only this but also assigns to each sentence the correct structural description.

affective meaning see **meaning**

affixing language A language which expresses grammatical relationships primarily through the use of affixes (sub-classified as **prefixes, suffixes, and infixes**). Surveys distinguish **prefixing languages**, such as Bantu, from **suffixing languages**, such as Latin. (See also **typology**.)

agglutinative language A language in which the words typically contain a linear sequence of formatives (roots and affixes), such as Turkish and Japanese. The notion contrasts with several other language types, referred to under **typology**.

allo- A prefix used when referring to any noticeable variation in the form of a linguistic unit which does not affect that unit's functional identity in the language – in other words, the variation does not cause a change of meaning. The most important applications are in the terms **allophone** (the variant forms of a **phoneme**) and allomorph (the variant forms of **morpheme**), but other uses of the notion will be found, such as allograph (the variant forms of a grapheme).

allograph see **allo-**

allokines see **kinesics**

allomorph see **allo-**

allophone see **allo-**

alternation The relationship which exists between the alternative forms (or variants) of a linguistic unit; usually symbolized by $\sim$. For example, the three main types of noun plural in English can be seen as variant forms conditioned by the nature of the preceding sound (they are **phonologically conditioned alternants**): /-s/ as in *cats*, /-z/ as in *dogs*, and /-iz/ as in *horses*. The notion has been especially used in morphology, where the term **morphemic alternant** is another way of expressing the idea of an allomorph. (See **allo-**.)

ambiguous Descriptive of any word or sentence which expresses more than one meaning. Two types of ambiguity are widely recognized. In grammatical (or structural) ambiguity, alternative interpretations can be assigned to a construction, as in *new cups and glasses*, which could mean either that the cups alone are new or that both the cups and the glasses are new. A sentence with more than two structural interpretations is said to be multiply (pronounced /'mʌltipliː/ ambiguous. In lexical ambiguity, alternative meanings can be assigned to an individual lexical item, as in *Look at that table*, where the word *table* could mean either an item of furniture or a set of figures.

analogy A process of regularization which affects the exceptional forms in the grammar of a language. Analogy can be seen in the short term, such as when young children are learning the irregular forms of their language and producing such utterances as *mices* and *goed*. Similar errors are found in foreign language learning. It can also be seen in the long term, in historical linguistics; Modern English *help*, for example, is now a regular verb (past tense *helped*), but was irregular in Old English.

analytic language A type of language in which words are invariable, and syntactic relationships are shown by word order. The notion is usually contrasted with a **synthetic language**, where words typically contain more than one morpheme. Many languages in south-east Asia, such as Chinese, are analytic languages. (See **typology**.)

anthropological linguistics A branch of linguistics which studies language variation and use in relation to human cultural patterns and beliefs. It has been especially concerned with non-Western languages, as found throughout the Americas, and has emphasized the ways in which these languages influence each other and can be grouped into types. The subject is sometimes distinguished from **linguistic anthropology**, a branch of anthropology which explores the place of language in the life of human communities.

applied linguistics A branch of linguistics where the primary concern is the application of linguistic theories, methods, and findings to the elucidation of language problems from other areas of experience. The most well-developed domain of applied linguistics is the teaching and learning of foreign languages. Other domains include the study of language disorders, translation and interpreting, lexicography, stylistics, and the use of the mother tongue in education. There is an uncertain boundary between applied linguistics and certain of the interdisciplinary branches of linguistics, such as sociolinguistics, which are also much concerned with practical outcomes (such as the development of a national language policy). However, the development of a theoretical foundation for these areas is in turn leading to a further use of the 'pure' vs 'applied' dichotomy, so that alongside sociolinguistics and psycholinguistics we now find **applied sociolinguistics** and **applied psycholinguistics**, defined analogously to the above.

applied pragmatics see **pragmatics**

appropriate Descriptive of any language variety or form which is considered to be suitable or possible in a given social situation. For example, contracted forms (such as *I'll*) and speech containing many assimilations and elisions (such as *gonna*) are appropriate to informal speech situations and inappropriate to formal speech situations. The purpose of the term is to provide an alternative to the absolute notion of correctness encountered in the **prescriptive** tradition of language study, where language forms were considered to be either 'right' or 'wrong', without regard to social context.

arbitrariness A suggested defining property of human language, when this is contrasted with the properties of other semiotic systems: language forms are said to lack any physical correspondence with the entities in the world to which they refer. For example, there is nothing in the pronunciation or structure of the word *chair* to reflect the shape, texture, or other properties of the object. There are a few exceptions – the onomatopoeic words in a language (such as *splash* and *murmur*) which do seem to reflect properties of the non-linguistic world.

areal linguistics The study of the linguistic properties of a geographically defined area (sometimes called a **Sprachbund**). The approach establishes linguistic areas, such as the Scandinavian languages, where it is possible to show certain linguistic features in common as a result of the proximity of the speech communities. These classifications sometimes cut across those made on purely historical (genetic) grounds: a linguistic area would contain languages belonging to more than one family, and show common traits not shared by all the members of at least one of those families. A contrast is sometimes drawn with non-areal studies, such as the properties of male vs female speech.

articulatory phonetics see **phonetics**

asterisked form (1) A linguistic construction which is unacceptable or ungrammatical, such as *These cat is outside*; also called a **starred form**. (2) In historical linguistics, a form which has been reconstructed, there being no direct written evidence for its existence; the forms of Proto-Indo-European are all reconstructed forms, and preceded by an asterisk to distinguish them from attested forms.

auditory phonetics see **phonetics**

auxiliary language A language which has been adopted by a speech community for international or intranational communication. Only a minority of the local community (and in some cases, none of them) may use it as a mother tongue. English or French are widely used as auxiliary languages in parts of Africa.

behaviourism A school of psychology which emphasizes the study of observable and measurable behaviour, encountered in linguistics in the approach of the American linguist Leonard **Bloomfield**. It is most noticeable in his behaviourist account of meaning in terms of observable stimuli and responses made by people in specific situations. The approach fell out of favour following the development of a mentalistic view of language within generative linguistics. (See also **mentalism**.)

biolinguistics A branch of linguistics which studies the biological preconditions for language development and use in human beings; also known as **biological linguistics**. The subject includes both long-term developments, to do with the history of language in the human race, and short-term developments, to do with the development of language in the individual.

Bloomfield, Leonard (1887–1949) US linguist known primarily from his book, *Language* (1933), which was the dominant influence on a whole generation of linguists. Bloomfieldianism was mainly characterized by its behaviouristic principles for the study of meaning, its insistence on rigorous discovery procedures for establishing linguistic units, and a general concern to make linguistics autonomous and scientific. It was a formative influence on **structural** linguistics. Its pre-eminence waned following the emergence of generative grammar in the late 1950s.

borrowing The process or result of adopting a linguistic form from another language or dialect; a lexical borrowing is often called a **loan word**. Examples include (from French to English) *restaurant* and (from English to French) *weekend*. Less commonly, grammatical features are borrowed, such as the use of English plural *-s* when European languages borrow such words as *drinks*, *girls*, and *ski-lifts*.

bound form see **morpheme**

broad transcription see **transcription**

case grammar An influential approach to grammatical analysis, devised in the late 1960s by US linguist Charles Fillmore (1929–). The approach recognizes a set of syntactic functions in the analysis of sentences, and gives these an interpretation in terms of semantic roles (such as agentive and locative).

child language acquisition see **acquisition**

Chomsky, (Avram) Noam (1928–) US linguist, Professor of Modern Languages and Linguistics at the Massachusetts Institute of Technology, whose theory of language known as transformational-generative grammar revolutionized work in linguistics in 1957, when his monograph *Syntactic Structures* was published.

Several of his later works introduced new directions into linguistic theory, notably *Aspects of the Theory of Syntax* (1965), *Language and Mind* (1968) and *Knowledge of Language* (1986). (See **generative grammar**.)

clinical linguistics A branch of linguistics in which linguistic theories, methods and findings are applied to the analysis of medical conditions or settings involving a disorder of language. This application involves linguists working in collaboration with speech pathologists and others in helping to assess, diagnose and remediate disorders of production or comprehension in spoken or written language. These studies take place in educational as well as clinical situations.

cognate A language or linguistic form which is historically derived from the same source as another language or form. The various Romance languages (French, Spanish, etc.) are cognate languages, as they all derive from Latin; and corresponding words (*mère*, *madre*, etc.) are cognate words.

cognitive meaning see **meaning**

communication The transmission of information (a 'message') between a source and a receiver, using a signalling system. The notion provides a broad frame of reference for studies of language, which can be viewed as just one type of signalling system, used by humans. Other types of signalling are used by animals, and some of these are available to humans (such as the non-verbal features of gesture and facial expression). The study of human communication (**semiotics**) also needs to take into account such factors as the feedback between participants, their intentions in communicating, and the interaction between different communicative modalities (auditory/vocal, visual, tactile). A major function of language is to communicate ideas, but it is not the only one: language may also be used in such areas as aesthetics (e.g., poetic metre), social rapport (e.g., conventional greetings), and play (e.g., children's ball-games), which do not involve the transmission of 'ideas' in any clear sense.

communicative competence A speaker's unconscious knowledge of the situational appropriateness of language, including such matters as where and when utterances are best used, and to what kind of person; also called pragmatic competence. The notion emerged in contrast with linguistic competence, the speaker's unconscious knowledge of the formal patterning of language. (See competence.)

comparative linguistics A branch of linguistics which makes statements concerning the characteristics of different languages (especially those believed to have a common origin) or different historical states of a language. The subject, with an exclusively historical emphasis, developed under the heading of comparative philology (or simply philology). One of its main techniques was the use of the comparative method – the comparison of forms taken from cognate languages to determine the nature of their historical relationship. Having developed in an era prior to the emergence of modern linguistics, comparative philology displays several differences of aim, emphasis and technique compared with the kind of comparative work which would be carried on within a framework of contemporary linguistic theory. A comparativist within a linguistics department would tend to be called a historical linguist, whereas the name philologist would tend to be reserved for a comparativist in a department of literature or modern languages. (See also linguistics.)

comparative philology see **comparative linguistics**

comparative reconstruction see **reconstruction**

competence A person's unconscious knowledge of his/her language – specifically, of the system of rules which has been mastered, enabling the person to produce and understand an indefinite number of sentences, and to recognize grammatical mistakes and ambiguities; it contrasts with **performance**. There are several derived notions. **Communicative** or pragmatic competence is the speaker's knowledge of the rules governing the appropriateness of sentences in social settings. Textual or discourse competence is the knowledge of the rules governing units longer than a single sentence. The term is also used in social, cognitive, and literary contexts.

competence grammar see **grammar**

component A major section of the organization of a **generative grammar**, such as the 'phrase-structure component' or the 'phonological component'. The application of the term varies between grammatical models. Further sub-divisions are referred to as sub-components.

computational linguistics A branch of linguistics in which computational techniques and concepts are applied to the elucidation of problems in linguistics and phonetics. Areas of application include the testing of grammars, automatic translation, speech analysis and synthesis, the use of large-scale statistical and concordancing techniques in literary and corpus studies, and the computational processing of text (**natural language** processing).

computer corpus see corpus

constituent A linguistic unit which is a component of a larger construction. The notion was first developed in relation to the process of constituent analysis, whereby sentences are progressively analysed into a series of hierarchically organized elements. The major divisions that can be made in a construction, at any level, are the immediate constituents (ICs) of that construction. The irreducible elements which result from this analysis are known as the ultimate constituents (UCs). For example, *The dog barked* has, as its ICs, *the dog* and *barked*. *The dog* has the ICs *the* and *dog*. *Barked* has the ICs *bark* and *-ed*. The UCs are *the*, *dog*, *bark* and *-ed*. The constituent structure of a sentence can be displayed using brackets or tree diagrams. A grammar which analyses sentences in this way is a constituency grammar.

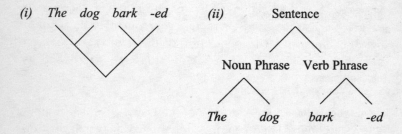

(iii)   *((The (dog)) (bark (ed)))*

Fig. 1   Three ways of showing the constituent structure of the sentence *The dog barked*

consultant see **informant**

context (1) The parts of a spoken or written utterance near or adjacent to a unit which is the focus of attention. The meaning of a word, for example, is clear only when it is seen in the context of neighbouring words (a process of **contextualization**). In **generative grammar**, the notion has been used as part of a classification of types of grammar. In a **context-free grammar**, the rules apply regardless of context: they are all of the type 'Rewrite X as Y' without further conditions. In a **context-sensitive** (or **context-restricted**) grammar, there are rules of the type 'Rewrite X as Y in the structural context of Z'. (2) The features of the non-linguistic world in relation to which linguistic units are systematically used; also called the **situational context**. The contextual meaning of an utterance, in this sense, is the use it has in its social context, taking into account such factors as the age, sex and location of the speaker.

context-free grammar see **context**

context-restricted grammar see **context**

context-sensitive grammar see **context**

contextual meaning see **meaning**

contextualization see **context**

contrast A difference between linguistic units, especially one which serves to distinguish meanings. Such differences are referred to as **distinctive, functional,** or **significant,** and may be found at any level of linguistic organization. Examples from English are the contrast between /t/ and /d/ (a phonological contrast), between *he is* and *is he* (a grammatical contrast), and between *fat* and *thin* (a lexical contrast).

conversation analysis The study of the methods people use to engage in conversation and other forms of spoken social interaction. The approach uses recordings of real conversations, and views verbal exchanges as a fundamental form of social organization.

Copenhagen School A group of linguists who constituted the Copenhagen Linguistics Circle in the mid-1930s, and who developed an approach to linguistics known as **glossematics**. Largely through its main theoretician, Louis Hjelmslev (1899–1965), the school developed a philosophical basis for linguistic theory which was not surpassed until the formalization introduced by **generative grammar**.

core grammar The universal set of linguistic principles which characterize all the **unmarked** grammatical principles found in language. A rule which conforms to these principles is a **core rule**. One which does not is a **non-core rule**. The notion contrasts with the **periphery** of a grammar, which contains the constructional properties specific to an individual language or speaker.

coreference Sameness of reference between two or more constituents of a sentence. In the sentence *I said I would resign*, the two *I*s are coreferential. In the sentence *He said he would resign*, there is ambiguity between the two *he*'s: the second *he* may or may not refer to the same person as the first. The ambiguity can be shown by using indices: *He$_i$ said he$_i$ would resign* vs *He$_i$ said he$_j$ would resign*.

core rule see **core grammar**

corpus A collection of linguistic data, either written texts or a transcription of recorded speech, which is used as a starting point of language description or as a way of verifying hypotheses about a language. A **computer corpus** is a large body of naturally occurring, machine-readable texts. **Corpus linguistics** deals with the principles and practice of using corpora in linguistic study.

correct see **appropriate**

counter-example A piece of data which falsifies a hypothesis about language, and which leads (or should lead) to the revision of an analysis. There is frequent discussion in linguistics over whether a suggested counter-example is important or not.

counter-intuitive An analysis which is implausible, according to the **intuition** of the native speaker of a language or of the linguist analysing the language. For example, an analysis which derives positive sentences from negative ones is felt to be less natural than one deriving negatives from positives.

creativity The capacity of language users to produce and understand an indefinitely large number of sentences, most of which they will not have heard or used before. The term is used to characterize the **productivity** of language, a finite set of rules being used to produce a potentially infinite number of sentences. The creation of new sentences in this way is considered to be a defining feature of human language; it is not a property of animal communication systems. Care must be taken not to confuse this sense of 'creative' with that found in artistic or literary contexts, where such notions as imagination and originality are crucial.

critical linguistics A developing branch of linguistics which aims to reveal the hidden power relations and ideological processes at work in spoken or written texts. The social context which gives rise to a text is considered an essential part of that text's interpretation.

cultural transmission A suggested defining property of human language, when this is contrasted with the properties of other semiotic systems, whereby the ability to speak a language is transmitted from generation to generation by a process of environmental learning, and not genetically. Such learning does not seem to be a crucial factor in animal systems of communication.

data Phenomena which constitute the subject matter of enquiry – in the case of linguistics, spoken, written, and signed language. There are two main views concerning the nature of linguistic data. In the traditional conception, linguistic data are the observable patterns found in a collection of textual material (such as would be encountered in a **corpus**). In the generative conception, the language user's judgements about the language are included as part of the data for analysis. (See **intuition**.)

decision procedure see **evaluation procedure**

deep structure In transformational grammar, the abstract syntactic representation of a sentence; it contrasts with **surface structure**. It is an underlying level of structural organization which specifies all the factors governing the way a sentence should be interpreted. In later linguistic theory, various developments of this basic notion have been introduced, along with fresh terminology (such as D-structure).

denotative meaning see **meaning**

dependency grammar A type of formal grammar developed in the 1950s, notably by the French linguist Lucien Tesnière (1893–1953). The approach establishes types of dependencies between the elements of a construction as a means of explaining grammatical relationships. Several kinds of dependency grammar have since been proposed.

derivation (1) In historical linguistics, the development of a linguistic form over time. Sounds, words, and structures are said to be derived from corresponding forms in an earlier state of a language. (2) A major category of word formation, the domain of derivational morphology. Derivational affixes, such as *-ship*, *-tion*, and *-ment* are used to form new words. (See **morphology**.) (3) In generative grammar, the set of formally identifiable stages used in generating a sentence, from an initial symbol to a terminal string. The derivation represents the whole set of rules which have been applied in order to generate the sentence.

derivational morphology see **derivation**; **morphology**

description A systematic, objective, precise and comprehensive account of the patterns and use of a particular language (dialect, variety, sample, etc.) at a particular point in time. Descriptive linguistics aims to account for the facts of linguistic usage as they are, and not how they ought to be, with reference to some imagined ideal state. In this respect, it thus adopts a different viewpoint from that of **prescriptive** grammar. Within linguistics, the emphasis on a given time places the subject in contrast with historical linguistics, where the aim is to demonstrate linguistic change. The emphasis on a particular language also differentiates the subject from several other aspects of linguistic enquiry, notably from general linguistics, where the aim is to make statements about 'language' as a whole.

descriptive adequacy see **adequacy**

descriptive grammar see **grammar**

developmental linguistics A branch of linguistics concerned with the study of the acquisition of language in children. The aim is to provide a description of patterns of development and an explanation of the norms and variations encountered, both within individual languages and universally. Because of the particular relevance of psychological factors, the subject is sometimes called **developmental psycholinguistics**.

diachronic linguistics The study of languages from the point of view of their development through time; also known as historical linguistics. This important concept was introduced by Ferdinand de **Saussure**, who saw it as a major dimension of language study. He contrasted it with **synchronic linguistics**, where languages are analysed without reference to their history. Until the twentieth century, most studies of language were diachronic in character, investigating long-term changes in pronunciation, grammar, or vocabulary, such as from Indo-European into Latin, from Germanic into English, or from Middle English into Modern English. After Saussure, the emphasis shifted away from the historical approach; modern linguistics became primarily a synchronic subject.

direct elicitation see **elicitation**

discourse A continuous stretch of (especially spoken) language larger than a sentence, often constituting a coherent unit, such as a sermon, argument, joke, or narrative. The attempt to discover linguistic regularities in discourse is carried on under the heading of discourse analysis or discourse linguistics. Discourse knowledge, in a broad sense, subsumes the whole set of norms, preferences and expectations which relate language to context, enabling users to produce and interpret the range of discourse units in a language.

discourse competence see **competence**

discovery procedure A set of techniques which can be automatically applied to a sample of language, which will produce a correct grammatical analysis. Attempts to develop such a procedure characterized the work of many Bloomfieldian linguists, and were strongly criticized in early formulations of **generative grammar**.

discreteness A suggested defining property of human language, when this is contrasted with the properties of other semiotic systems, whereby the elements of a signal can be analysed as having definable boundaries, with no gradation or continuity between them. The term is especially used in phonetics and phonology for sounds which have relatively clear-cut boundaries within the stream of speech. A system lacking discreteness is said to be **non-discrete**.

displacement A suggested defining property of human language, when this is contrasted with the properties of other semiotic systems, whereby language can be used to refer to contexts removed from the immediate situation of the speaker (as in the case of tenses which refer to past or future time). Animal calls seem generally tied to specific situations, such as danger and hunger, and have nothing comparable to displaced speech.

distinctiveness see **contrast**

distribution The total set of linguistic contexts in which a unit can occur. A distributional analysis plots the places in larger linguistic units where smaller units occur. Examples include the distribution of phonemes within the syllable, of morphemes within the word, and of words within the sentence.

double articulation see **duality of structure**

D-structure see **deep structure**

duality of structure A suggested defining property of human language, which sees language as structurally organized in terms of two abstract levels; also called (after the French linguist, André Martinet (1908–) **double articulation**. At one (higher) level, language is organized in terms of meaningful units (such as morphemes and words); at the other (lower) level, language is organized as a sequence of segments which lack any meaning in themselves, but which combine to form units of meaning.

dynamic linguistics The study of language variation from a temporal point of view. The synchronic states of a language are seen in terms of the various processes of change which produce and affect them, such as the relative rate of a change as it moves in various directions through a speech community.

educational linguistics A branch of linguistics which applies the theories, methods, and findings of linguistics primarily to the study of the teaching and learning of a native language, in both spoken and written forms, in schools or other educational settings; also called **pedagogical linguistics**. It includes such topics as the study of reading and writing, language variety across the curriculum, and the teaching of grammar.

E-language An abbreviation for **externalized language**, a term proposed by Noam **Chomsky** to refer to a collection of sentences understood independently of the properties of the mind; contrasted with **I-language**. It subsumes the notion of language as a system of forms paired with meanings, which it is the purpose of a grammar to describe.

elicitation The technique of obtaining reliable linguistic data from speakers (**informants**) – either actual utterances or judgements about utterances; also called **direct elicitation**. Considerable attention is paid to devising ways of eliciting information so that the informant can respond unselfconsciously.

emic/etic A pair of terms which characterize opposed approaches to the study of linguistic data. An etic approach is one where the physical patterns of language are described with a minimum of reference to their function within the language system, as in phonetic and graphetic analysis. An emic approach takes full account of all functional relationships, setting up a system of abstract contrastive units as the basis of description, as in graphemic and phonemic analysis. The distinction is a central feature of the approach to language devised by the US linguist Kenneth Pike (1912–).

equivalence A relationship of equality of power among grammars. Grammars which generate the same set of sentences are said to demonstrate **weak equivalence**. Grammars which not only generate the same set of sentences but also assign the same structural descriptions to each are said to demonstrate **strong equivalence**. Grammars which generate different sentences or structural descriptions are **non-equivalent**.

état de langue ('state of language') A language seen at a particular point in time, regardless of its antecedents or later development – the primary subject matter of **synchronic linguistics**. The term was introduced into linguistics by Ferdinand de **Saussure**.

ethnography of speaking/communication see **ethnolinguistics**

ethnolinguistics A branch of linguistics which studies language in relation to its cultural context, often subsuming the concerns of **anthropological linguistics**. The phrases **ethnography of speaking** or **ethnography of communication** are used for the ethnographic study of language as a social institution, especially by participant observation of naturally occurring discourse in its cultural and social context.

etymology The study of the origins and history of the form and meaning of words; a branch of historical linguistics. A **folk etymology** occurs when a word is assumed to come from a particular source, because of some association of form and meaning, whereas in fact it has a different derivation (e.g., the use of *sparrow-grass* for *asparagus*).

evaluation procedure A technique which provides criteria for choosing between alternative analyses of a set of data; for example,

extralinguistic

one analysis might be simpler or more elegant than another. A relativistic notion of this kind is thought to be more realistic than that involved in a **decision procedure**, which is a technique that could be automatically applied to a series of grammars of a language, to decide which was the best grammar. The latter goal is held to be impossible to achieve, in our present state of linguistic knowledge.

explanatory adequacy see **adequacy**

exponence The relationship of correspondence between linguistic units at a higher level of analysis and those at a lower level. For example, **morphemes** are said to have phonological units as their exponents, and the exponents of the latter are phonetic features.

expressive meaning see **meaning**

extended standard theory (EST) A model of **generative grammar** which developed in the early 1970s out of that expounded in Noam Chomsky's *Aspects of the Theory of Syntax* (1965) – known as the **standard theory**. The 'extension' is primarily due to the range of the semantic rules, some of which were allowed to operate with surface structure as input.

externalized language see **E-language**

extralinguistic (1) Descriptive of anything in the world (other than language) in relation to which language is used – the extralinguistic situation. (2) Descriptive of properties of communication that are not clearly analysable in linguistic terms, such as gestures and tones of voice. The term **paralinguistic** is often used in this sense.

family of languages A set of languages deriving from a common ancestor, or 'parent'. An example is the Indo-European family, which consists of such 'daughter' languages as Sanskrit, Greek and Latin. The family tree was devised by nineteenth-century philologists in order to represent these relationships.

family tree see **family of languages**

feedback The process whereby the sender of a message obtains a reaction from the receiver which enables a check to be made on the efficiency of the **communication**. Speakers are also able to monitor their own performance, both by observing the reactions of others and by sensing what is happening (e.g., their own loudness level and articulatory movements) while they speak.

finite-state grammar A simple kind of **generative grammar**, which generates sentences by working through a sentence from left to right. An initial element is selected, and thereafter the possibilities of occurrence of all other elements are wholly determined by the nature of the elements preceding them.

first language see **native speaker**

Firth, J(ohn) R(upert) (1890–1960) British linguist, Professor of General Linguistics in the University of London between 1944 and 1956, who was a formative influence on the development of linguistics in Great Britain. Many of his ideas were developed by a neo-Firthian group of scholars, whose main theoretician is M. A. K. **Halliday** (1925–).

folk etymology see **etymology**

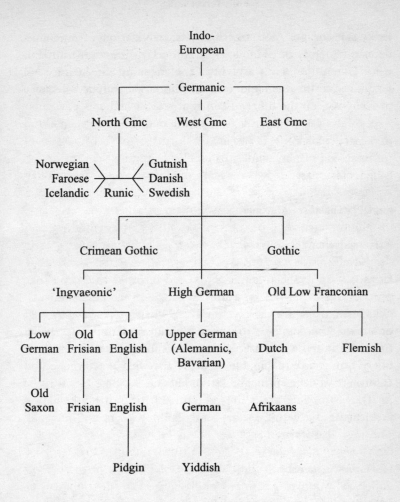

Fig. 2 **The Germanic family of languages**

form (1) The abstract structural characterization of language, defined in terms of phonology, graphology, grammar and lexicon. The notion contrasts with the meaning or function of language, on the one hand, and the phonic or graphic substance of language, on the other. (2) A unit established at a particular level of analysis (a **linguistic form**) or the realization of such a unit in a particular context (as in the 'forms of a verb'). A set of forms which display similar or identical grammatical features is called a **form class**.

formal grammar see **grammar**

formal universal see **universal**

formalism An artificial language devised in order to characterize precisely an artificial or a natural language. In theoretical linguistics, formalisms are mainly used in a descriptive way, to help define the grammatical properties of a natural language. When a linguistic analysis is **formalized**, the rules and other factors governing the analysis are capable of being specified in a precise and rigorous way. In principle, it ought to be possible for the analysis to be interpreted in the terms of logic or mathematics. A formalized account, in this sense, is opposed to an 'informal' one. (See also **grammar** (1).)

free form see **morpheme**

function (1) The relationship between a linguistic form and other parts of the sentence (or larger unit) in which it is used. For example, a noun phrase is said to function as the subject or object of a sentence; the **phoneme** /h/ can function initially but not finally in a syllable in English. Any elements which contrast within a system are said to have a function within that system. The use made of a linguistic contrast in a system is called its functional load or yield. A functionalist approach is one where the notion of function (which can be defined in various ways) is treated as central. (2) The relationship between a linguistic form and the social or interpersonal setting in which it is used. For example, the functions of language are said to include the communication of ideas, the expression of attitudes, the promotion of social rapport, and so on.

functional load see **function**

functional sentence perspective A theory of linguistic analysis associated with the modern exponents of the **Prague School** of linguistics. It is an analysis of utterances or texts in terms of the information they contain, the role of each **utterance** part being evaluated for its semantic contribution to the whole.

functional yield see **function**

functionalist see **function**

fusional language A type of language in which words typically contain more than one **morpheme**, but there is no one-to-one correspondence between these morphemes and the linear sequence of morphs the words contain; also known as an **inflecting language**. Examples include Sanskrit and Latin. The notion contrasts with several other language types, referred to under **typology**.

general linguistics An approach to **linguistics** where the emphasis is on the universal applicability of theory and method in the study of languages. The term is usually contrasted with the more particular concerns of applied and descriptive linguistics.

general phonetics see **phonetics**

general pragmatics see **pragmatics**

generalized phrase-structure grammar (GPSG) A linguistic theory which was developed in the 1980s as an alternative to transformational accounts of language, providing a framework for writing fully explicit formal grammars for natural languages. GPSGs are weakly equivalent to a class of context-free **phrase-structure grammars**.

generative grammar A grammar that defines the set of grammatical sentences in a language. Formal rules project a finite set of sentences upon the potentially infinite set which constitutes the language as a whole, doing this in an explicit manner, assigning to each sentence a structural description. The term is also used for the school of thought which expounds this approach, introduced by Noam **Chomsky** in *Syntactic Structures* (1957). The two main branches of generative linguistics are **generative phonology** and **generative syntax**.

genetic classification The classification of languages on the basis of the hypothesis that they have a common origin. The approach makes use of the model of a family tree, which displays the relative chronology and closeness of relationship of a group of languages. (See also **comparative linguistics**; **typology**.)

geographical linguistics A branch of linguistics which studies languages and dialects in terms of their regional distribution; more usually referred to as **areal linguistics**.

geolinguistics A branch of linguistics which studies the geographical distribution of languages throughout the world, with reference to their political, economic and cultural status. The term is also used more narrowly, for an approach to dialectology which makes use of the insights of **sociolinguistics**.

glossematics see **Copenhagen School**

government and binding theory (GB) A model of **generative grammar** developed by Noam **Chomsky** in the early 1980s, deriving from **extended standard theory**. It recognizes three main levels of structure (D-structure, S-structure and Logical Form) and a set of interacting sub-theories, two of which (the Government sub-theory and the Binding sub-theory) give the approach its name. GB is commonly described as a modular theory, because of the way its explanations derive from different principles (modules) of the grammar. It is also suggested that essentially the same principles of syntax are operative in all languages, although they can take a slightly different form in different languages. For this reason, the theory is often referred to as the **principles and parameters** approach.

grammar (1) An analysis of the structure of a language, either as encountered in a corpus of speech or writing (a **performance grammar**) or as predictive of a speaker's knowledge (a **competence grammar**). A contrast is often drawn between a **descriptive grammar**, which provides a precise account of actual usage, and a **prescriptive grammar**, which tries to establish rules for the correct use of language in society. A further contrast may be drawn between a grammar which concentrates on the study of linguistic forms (formal grammar) and one which assumes the existence of extralinguistic categories in order to define grammatical units (notional grammar). A comprehensive practical handbook of the structure of a language is a reference grammar. **Traditional grammar** refers to the range of attitudes and methods found in the pre-linguistic era of grammatical study. (2) An analysis of the structural properties which define human language (a universal grammar). Theoretical grammar, in this context, goes beyond the study of individual languages, using linguistic data as a means of developing insights into the nature of language as such, and into the categories and processes needed for linguistic analysis. The formalized techniques of logic and mathematics may also be used as part of the analysis, and this too is referred to as formal grammar. (3) A level of structural organization which can be studied independently of phonology and semantics. It is generally sub-divided into the domains of syntax and morphology.

grammar induction see **learnability**

grammatical ambiguity see **ambiguous**

grammaticality The conformity of a sentence, or part of a sentence, to the rules defined by a particular grammar of the language; also called well-formedness. A preceding asterisk indicates that the sentence is incapable of being accounted for by the rules of the grammar (i.e. it is ungrammatical or ill-formed). The distinction between grammaticality and **acceptability** should be kept in mind: a sentence may be well-formed but nonetheless unacceptable (e.g., it might not make sense). Also, in this context no social judgement is implied by calling a sentence grammatical or ungrammatical. A rather different use of the term is found in the context of **prescriptive** grammar where, for example, *I haven't done nothing* would be said to be ungrammatical because the double negative does not conform to the canons of the standard language.

graphemes see **graphology**

graphic substance see **substance**

graphology The study of the writing system of a language, or the writing system itself – a domain which has developed on analogy with **phonology**. The approach aims to establish the minimal contrastive units of visual language (**graphemes**) on the basis of an analysis of the properties of graphic substance (stroke direction and size, spacing, colour, layout, etc.).

Halliday, M(ichael) A(lexander) K(irkwood) (1925–) British linguist, based in Australia in recent years, whose theoretical work in the 1950s and 1960s took further several of the ideas of J. R. **Firth**. He is the originator of **scale-and-category** grammar and, later, **systemic grammar**.

head parameter see **parameter**

hierarchy A classification of linguistic units which recognizes a series of successively subordinate levels. For example, a sentence can be seen to 'consist of' a series of clauses, which in turn consist of phrases, which consist of words, which consist of **morphemes**.

historical linguistics see **comparative linguistics; diachronic linguistics**

iconicity A suggested defining property of some **semiotic** systems, but not human language, to refer to signals whose physical form closely corresponds to characteristics of the entities in the world to which they refer. This is the normal state of affairs in animal communication. In language, only a small number of items are directly symbolic (**iconic**) in this way, such as onomatopoeic expressions (*cuckoo*, *murmur*, etc.).

idealization The ignoring of certain aspects of the variability found in linguistic data, in order to arrive at an analysis which is as generally applicable as possible. The notion is part of the definition of linguistic **competence**, which assumes an 'ideal speaker-hearer' in an ideal (i.e. homogeneous) speech community, who is unaffected by memory limitations, distractions, and other problems when using the language.

ideational meaning see **meaning**

idiolect The linguistic system of an individual person. The notion is seen in contrast with the shared local features of language which constitute a regional, social, occupational or other dialect.

I-language An abbreviation for internalized language, a term proposed by Noam **Chomsky** to refer to language viewed as an element of a person's mind; it contrasts with **E-language**.

ill-formedness see **grammaticality**

immediate constituent (IC) analysis The analysis of a syntactic construction into its major parts (**constituents**), the subsequent divisions being themselves analysed into their major parts until irreducible constituents are reached. The technique was a major feature of structuralist linguistics, as propounded by Leonard **Bloomfield**.

incorporating language A type of language which uses long, morphologically complex word forms; also called a **polysynthetic language**. Many American Indian languages are of this type. The notion contrasts with several other language types, referred to under **typology**.

indeterminacy A state of affairs in linguistic analysis where there is uncertainty on the part of a native speaker, or disagreement between native speakers, as to what is grammatical or acceptable. The uncertainty may also be on the part of a linguist, or between several linguists, as to how or where a boundary line between different types of structure might best be drawn.

inflecting language A type of language where words display grammatical relationships morphologically, using a system of prefixes, suffixes or infixes. Examples include Latin, Greek and Arabic. The notion contrasts with several other language types, referred to under **typology**.

inflectional morphology see **morphology**

informant Someone who acts as a source of data for linguistic analysis, usually a native speaker of a language. Informants provide samples of spoken, written or signed language, and also make judgements about the acceptability of sentences. In recent years, some linguists have preferred to use the term **consultant**, reflecting the collaborative nature of the work.

innateness hypothesis The view that a child is born with a biological predisposition to learn language. It argues that the rapid and complex development of children's grammatical competence can be explained only by the hypothesis that they are born with an innate knowledge of at least some of the universal structural principles of human language. The view is primarily to be found within generative linguistics.

institutional linguistics A developing branch of linguistics in which the focus is on the language used in professional contexts, such as the 'institutions' of law, medicine, education, business, and religion.

interchangeability A suggested defining property of a semiotic system, when this is contrasted with the properties of other semiotic systems, which refers to the system's ability to be mutually transmitted and received by members of the same species. Not all animal signals have this property; for example, some female calls are not shared by male members of the species.

internal reconstruction see **reconstruction**

internalization The process whereby speakers come to possess knowledge of the structure of their language. The term is primarily used in the context of language **acquisition**, where children or foreign learners are said to 'internalize' rules (such as the rule for forming a regular past tense by adding -*ed*).

internalized language see **I-language**

intuition, linguistic The knowledge we have about our own language; also known as **tacit knowledge** or **Sprachgefühl**. Using their linguistic intuition, native speakers can make decisions about whether a sentence is acceptable or not, how sentences relate to each other (e.g., statements and questions), how words relate in meaning to each other (e.g., as opposites or synonyms), and whether particular sound sequences are possible (e.g., *str* is possible in English, but *srt* is not). The importance of using intuition in analysing a language was emphasized by Noam **Chomsky**, and became an important tenet of **generative grammar**.

irregular Descriptive of a linguistic form which is an exception to the pattern stated by a rule. For example, nouns such as *mice* and *geese* are irregular, because they do not follow the rule which forms a plural by adding -*s*. Grammar is concerned with the discovery of regular patterns in linguistic data; irregularities are usually handled by incorporating the exceptional information into a dictionary. (See also **regular**.)

isolating language A type of language in which words are typically invariable, and syntactic relationships are primarily shown by word order. Examples include Chinese, Vietnamese, and many languages of south-east Asia. An alternative is to describe these languages as **analytic**. The notion contrasts with several other language types, referred to under **typology**.

Junggrammatiker see **neogrammarians**

kineme see **kinesics**

kinesics The study of the systematic use of facial expression and body gesture to communicate meaning, especially when this relates to the use of language (as when a smile alters the interpretation of a sentence). Kinesic behaviour is usually analysed in **emic** terms, as kinemes, allokines, etc.

language (1) The act of speaking, writing or signing, in a given situation; often referred to by the French term **parole**. (2) The linguistic system underlying a person's use of speech, writing or sign (often referred to as **competence**); more generally, the system underlying the shared spoken, written or signed behaviour of a whole community (often referred to by the French term **langue**). (3) The biological faculty enabling individuals to learn and use speech, writing or sign – a defining feature of human behaviour. (4) A particular variety or level of speech, writing or sign – as encountered in such phrases as 'religious language' and 'bad language'. (5) An artificially constructed system used to expound a conceptual area (e.g., a 'computer language') or to facilitate communication (an 'artificial language'); in this sense the term contrasts with a **natural language**.

language acquisition device (LAD) see **acquisition**

langue A term introduced by Ferdinand de **Saussure** to refer to the language system shared by a community of speakers. It is contrasted with parole, which is the concrete act of speaking in actual situations by an individual. **Competence** and **performance** are analogous notions within generative linguistics.

learnability A suggested defining property of human language, referring to the way any language can be acquired by a normal child given the opportunity to do so. Learnability **theory** is a mathematical theory which deals with idealized learning procedures for acquiring grammars on the basis of exposure to evidence about languages. It is also called learning theory or grammar induction.

learnability theory see **learnability**

learning see **acquisition**

learning theory see **learnability**

level (1) A major dimension of the structural organization of language, held to be susceptible of independent study. The most widely recognized levels are **phonology, grammar** (or **syntax**) and **semantics**, but other divisions and sub-divisions have also been called levels, such as **morphology, phonetics**, and **pragmatics**. (2) In **generative grammar**, a type of representation encountered within the derivation of a sentence. The chief example is the distinction between the levels of **deep structure** and **surface structure**. (3) A structural layer within a **hierarchy**. For example, the notions of sentence, clause, phrase, word and morpheme can be described as different grammatical levels.

lexeme The minimal distinctive unit in the **lexicon** of a language; also called a **lexical item**. The term was introduced in order to avoid the ambiguity of the term word, when discussing vocabulary. A lexeme may consist of more than one word, as in such phrasal verbs as *come up with*.

lexical ambiguity see **ambiguous**

lexical entries see **lexicon**

lexical-functional grammar (LFG) A linguistic theory, developed in the 1980s, in which the role of the **lexicon** is considered to be central, and grammar is primarily analysed in terms of syntactic **functions**.

lexical item see **lexeme**

lexical morphology see **morphology**

lexical phonology see **lexicon**

lexical syntax see **lexicon**

lexicography see **lexicon**

lexicology see **lexicon**

lexicon The vocabulary of a language, seen as a set of lexical items listed in a dictionary in the form of lexical entries; sometimes called lexis. In **generative grammar**, the lexicon is the component containing all the information about the structural properties of lexical items. Several approaches attach particular importance to the lexicon. In lexical syntax, syntactic rules are incorporated within the lexicon. In lexical phonology, some of the phonological rules are transferred to the lexicon, within the morphological component. The study of a language's lexicon is carried on by lexicology, a subject which should be distinguished from lexicography, the art and science of dictionary-making.

lexis see **lexicon**

linguist A student or practitioner of the subject of linguistics. The term linguistician is never used by professional linguists about themselves. It is important to be aware of the possibility of confusion with the earlier and still current sense of someone proficient in several languages.

linguistic anthropology see **anthropological linguistics**

linguistic competence see **communicative competence**

linguistic determinism see **linguistic relativity**

linguistic form see **form**

linguistic philosophy see **philosophical linguistics**

linguistic relativity A view of the relationship between language and culture, or between language and thought, which asserts that language determines the way people perceive and organize their worlds (linguistic determinism). Speakers of different languages, it is claimed, necessarily adopt different concepts of reality. The view is also called the **Sapir–Whorf Hypothesis**, after its first proponents, the US anthropological linguists Edward Sapir (1884–1939) and Benjamin Lee Whorf (1897–1941).

linguistic science(s) see **linguistics**

linguistic universal see **universal**

linguistician see **linguist**

linguistics The scientific study of language; also called linguistic science or (if phonetics is seen as a distinct domain) sciences. Several branches and approaches can be distinguished, according to the linguist's focus and range of interest. (See also **anthropological linguistics; applied linguistics; biolinguistics; clinical linguistics; comparative linguistics; computational linguistics; corpus; critical linguistics; developmental linguistics; diachronic linguistics; dynamic linguistics; educational linguistics; ethnolinguistics; general linguistics; institutional linguistics; mathematical linguistics; neurolinguistics; philosophical linguistics; poetics; psycholinguistics; quantitative linguistics; sociolinguistics; statistical linguistics; stylistics; synchronic linguistics; taxonomic linguistics; typology.**)

literary linguistics see **stylistics**

literary stylistics see **stylistics**

loan word see **borrowing**

manifestation see **realization**

marked see **markedness**

markedness An analytic principle whereby pairs of linguistic features, seen as oppositions, are given values of positive (marked) vs negative or neutral (unmarked). The principle can be interpreted in several ways, such as with reference to the presence or absence of a particular characteristic (e.g., an inflectional ending, such as plural, being the marked form of a noun) or to frequency of occurrence (the more frequent form being seen as unmarked). In recent generative linguistics, markedness theory deals with the tendencies of linguistic properties to be found in all languages: an unmarked property accords with these tendencies; a marked property goes against them.

markedness theory see **markedness**

Massachusetts Institute of Technology see **MIT**

mathematical linguistics A branch of linguistics which studies the mathematical properties of language, usually employing concepts of a statistical or algebraic kind. Areas of interest include the study of the formal properties of grammars, the exploration of parsing algorithms, and the investigation of the statistical properties of texts, in such fields as **stylistics** and **comparative linguistics**.

meaning A basic notion in linguistics, used both as a datum (the idea of 'signification' or 'interpretation') and as a criterion of analysis (the idea of 'contrastiveness' or 'distinctiveness'). The meaning of language can be studied from several complementary points of view. When language is seen to relate to the external world, terms such as referential or denotative meaning are used. When language relates to the mental states of speakers, the emotional aspects are identified under such headings as affective or expressive meaning, and the intellectual aspects under such headings as cognitive or ideational meaning. Variations in the extralinguistic situation can influence the way language is to be interpreted, and these are handled under such headings as contextual or situational meaning. The branch of linguistics with specific responsibility for the investigation of meaning is **semantics**.

medium A functionally distinct dimension in which a message is transmitted. In language, the two basic media are speech and writing, with signing a further option in certain cases (chiefly in deaf communication). The structural and functional differences between spoken and written language provide linguistics with an important topic of investigation.

mentalism A school of psychology which emphasizes the existence of mental states and processes independently of behaviour, and can explain behaviour. Its influence is to be seen primarily in the work of Noam **Chomsky**, especially in relation to **competence** and child language acquisition (the **innateness hypothesis**). Mentalistic linguistics can be seen in contrast to the **behaviourism** characteristic of earlier work in structuralist linguistics.

metalanguage A higher-level language devised in order to talk about an object of study (the **object language**). Linguistic metalanguage includes all the terminology, nomenclature and special expressions which have been introduced to talk about human language. Metalanguage is what this book and the others in this series are all about.

MIT The abbreviation of **Massachusetts Institute of Technology**, associated with the generative school of linguistic thought launched by Noam **Chomsky** in the late 1950s.

modularity see **government and binding theory**

monogenesis The hypothesis that all human languages originate from a single source. The alternative view is known as **polygenesis**. These terms are also used in **sociolinguistics**, as part of the discussion of the history of pidgins and creoles.

Montague grammar A linguistic theory derived from the work of US logician Richard Montague (1930–70), based on the semantics of formal (logical) languages. The grammar contains a syntactic and a semantic component related by a one-to-one correspondence between categories set up at the two levels.

morph see **morpheme**

morpheme The minimal distinctive unit of grammar, and the central concern of **morphology**. Morphemes are commonly classified into **free forms** (morphemes which can occur as separate words) and **bound forms** (morphemes which cannot so occur – mainly the affixes). Morphemes are abstract units, which are realized in speech or writing as discrete items (**morphs**). Morphemic variants (such as the different realizations of the English plural morpheme as /-s/, /-z/, and /-iz/) are called **allomorphs**.

morphemic alternant see **alternation**

morphemics see **morphology**

morphology The branch of grammar which studies the structure of words; it contrasts with **syntax**, which studies the way words combine into sentences. It is divided into the study of grammatical inflections (**inflectional morphology**) and the study of the processes of word formation (**lexical** or **derivational morphology**). When the emphasis is on the technique of analysing words into morphemes, especially as practised by US structuralist linguists in the 1940s and 1950s, the term **morphemics** is often used.

morphonology see **morphophonemics**

morphophonemics A branch of linguistics which analyses the phonological factors that determine the shape of **morphemes** or, alternatively, the grammatical factors that determine the shape of **phonemes**. For example, there is a special relationship between the phonemes /f/ and /v/ in English when these are seen in the context of noun plural formation (*knife/knives*, *leaf/leaves*, etc.). Morphophonemics is the preferred US term; in the European tradition, the preferred term is morphophonology or (especially in Eastern Europe) morphonology.

morphophonology see **morphophonemics**

morphosyntax A branch of linguistics which studies those grammatical categories for whose definition criteria of **morphology** and **syntax** both apply. Examples include the categories of number, person, and voice. The analysis of voice, for example, requires reference to morphology (inflectional endings on nouns and verbs) and syntax (word order).

morphotactics see **taxis**

narrow transcription see **transcription**

native language see **native speaker**

native speaker Someone for whom a particular language is a mother tongue (also called a native language or first language). The implication is that this language, having been acquired naturally during childhood, will be the one about which the speaker will have the most reliable intuitions. Linguists therefore generally try to find native-speaking informants, when investigating languages.

natural language A language used in ordinary human communication, as opposed to the theoretical or artificial systems used in such fields as computing and artificial intelligence. Natural language processing is a branch of computational linguistics which deals with the computational processing of textual materials in natural languages. Its applications include such areas as machine translation and literary text analysis.

natural language processing see **natural language**

neo-Firthian see **Firth, J. R.**

neogrammarians A nineteenth-century school of thought in comparative philology, initiated by the German scholars K. Brugmann (1848–1919) and S. A. Leskien (1840–1916). Their main tenet was that the sound laws set up to account for language change admitted no exceptions. The name comes from a translation of German Junggrammatiker ('young grammarians'), applied to the group by older scholars who objected to the forceful way in which this view was promulgated.

neurolinguistics A branch of linguistics which studies the neurological basis of language development and use, and attempts to construct a model of the brain's control over the processes of speaking, listening, reading, writing, and signing; also called neurological linguistics. It has been particularly concerned with such matters as articulatory timing and sequencing in speech production, and the nature of language breakdowns and disorders.

neurological linguistics see **neurolinguistics**

non-areal linguistics see **areal linguistics**

non-core rule see **core grammar**

non-discrete see **discreteness**

non-equivalent see **equivalence**

non-segmental phonology see **phonology**

non-verbal communication see **communication**

normative grammar see **normative rule**

normative rule A linguistic rule which is considered to set a socially approved standard of correctness for language use. Examples in English include such **prescriptive** rules as the use of *whom* (as opposed to *who*) in such sentences as *That's the lady whom I saw*, and such proscriptive rules as the banning of split infinitives (*to boldly go*). A systematic collection of such rules constitutes a normative grammar – a phenomenon which developed in the late eighteenth century, and is still widespread today.

notation see **transcription**

notional grammar see **grammar** (1)

null element see **zero**

object language see **metalanguage**

observational adequacy see **adequacy**

order The pattern of relationships comprising or underlying a linear sequence of linguistic units, as encountered in such notions as word order. In **generative grammar**, the term is used for the application of the rules of a grammar in a particular sequence.

paradigm see **paradigmatic relations**

paradigmatic relations The set of substitutional relationships which a linguistic unit has with other units, in a specific context; opposed to **syntagmatic relations**. These relations can be established at all levels of analysis. In phonology, for example, the relationship between /p/, /b/, /s/, etc. is paradigmatic in the context /—in/. In grammar, there is a paradigmatic relationship between *the*, *a*, *some*, etc. in the context — *cake*. The term paradigm is used more narrowly in grammar for the set of grammatically conditioned forms which are all derived from a single stem – as in the different cases of a Latin noun.

paralinguistic see **extralinguistic**

parameter In **government and binding theory**, a specification of the variations that a principle of grammar manifests among different languages. For example, a **head parameter** specifies the positions of heads within phrases. Determining the values of parameters for given languages is called **parameter-setting**.

parameter-setting see **parameter**

paraphrase The process or result of producing alternative versions of a sentence or text without changing its meaning. A sentence may have several paraphrases; for example, *The cat chased the mouse*, *The mouse was chased by the cat*, *It's the mouse that the cat chased.*

parole see **langue**

parsing In traditional grammar, the pedagogical exercise of labelling the grammatical elements of a sentence. In linguistics, parsing is more concerned with the criteria of analysis which led to the identification of these elements in the first place – how we know that a word is an adjective or a noun, for example. The term is now widely employed for the general process of analysis used in **computational linguistics**, where a text may be parsed in terms of syntactic, semantic and other kinds of information.

pedagogical linguistics see **educational linguistics**

perception see **speech perception**

performance Language seen as a set of specific utterances, as encountered in a corpus; it contrasts with **competence**, and is analogous to the Saussurean concept of parole. The study of performance includes such features as hesitations and unfinished structures, arising out of the biological, psychological and social constraints imposed on the speaker-hearer. These features must be discounted by any grammar which deals with the systematic processes of sentence construction. They may, however, be the focus of attention in a **performance grammar**.

performance grammar see **grammar**

periphery see **core grammar**

philology see **comparative linguistics**

philosophical linguistics A branch of linguistics which studies the role of language in relation to the understanding and elucidation of philosophical concepts, as well as the philosophical status of linguistic theories, methods, observations, and applications. Within philosophy, the corresponding interest is known as linguistic philosophy or the philosophy of language.

philosophical semantics see **semantics**

philosophy of language see **philosophical linguistics**

phoneme The minimal unit in the sound system of a language, according to traditional phonological theory (phonemic phonology or phonemics). The symbols of a phonemic transcription are placed between oblique brackets: /p/, /e/, etc. Variant forms of a phoneme are called allophones.

phonemic phonology see **phoneme**

phonemic transcription see **transcription**

phonemics see **phoneme**

phonetic transcription see **transcription**

phonetic universal see **phonetics**

phonetics The study of the production, transmission and reception of speech sounds. The three main branches of the subject reflect this definition: articulatory phonetics, acoustic phonetics and auditory phonetics. The name general phonetics reflects the subject's aim of discovering universal principles governing the nature and use of speech sounds. A phonetic universal is a feature of pronunciation shared by all languages, resulting from the same underlying processes of speech production or perception.

phonic substance see **substance**

phonologically conditioned alternants see **alternation**

phonology The study of the sound system of a language, or the sound system itself, and of the rules that operate within it; at a more general level, the comparative study of the sound systems of groups of languages, and ultimately of human language as a whole. It is usually viewed as an independent level or component of language organization, distinct from phonetics, grammar and semantics. Segmental phonology analyses speech into a series of discrete segments (vowels, consonants, syllables); suprasegmental or non-segmental phonology analyses features which extend over more than one segment (such as intonation and rhythm).

phonotactics see **taxis**

phrase structure see **structural**

phrase-structure grammar (PSG) A type of grammar which can generate not only strings of linguistic elements but also a **constituent** analysis of these strings. In a transformational grammar, as outlined by Noam **Chomsky** in *Syntactic Structures* (1957), the phrase-structure component uses a set of phrase-structure rules (PS rules) which specifies the hierarchical structure of a sentence, the linear sequence of its constituents, and, indirectly, some types of syntactic relations. Grammars have also been developed which are equivalent to PSGs but which do not employ PS rules, such as **generalized phrase-structure grammar**.

phrase-structure (PS) rules see **phrase-structure grammar**

poetics A branch of linguistics which studies those aspects of language which make a verbal message a work of art. The subject is chiefly concerned with literary texts (notably, poetry, as the name suggests), but it does not exclude the study of the aesthetic properties of other kinds of spoken or written language.

polygenesis see **monogenesis**

polysynthetic language see **incorporating language**

position A functionally contrastive place within a linguistic unit, usually defined as initial, medial or final. The notion can be used with reference to any level of analysis, but is most commonly encountered when talking about sounds within syllables and words, and about words within clauses and sentences.

pragmatic competence see **communicative competence**

pragmatics The study of language from the point of view of the users, especially of the choices they make, the constraints they encounter in using language in social interaction, and the effects their use of language has on the other participants in an act of communication. **General pragmatics** is the study of the principles governing the communicative use of language, especially as encountered in conversations. **Applied pragmatics** is the study of verbal interaction in such domains as counselling, medical interviews, and judicial sessions, where problems of communication are of critical importance. Several other terms will be encountered, as people strive to make sense of what is a relatively new and inchoate domain.

Prague School The views and methods of the Linguistic Circle of Prague, and of the scholars it influenced. The Circle was founded in 1926 by Vilém Mathesius (1882–1946) and included such linguists as Roman Jakobsen (1896–1983) and Nikolai Trubetskoy (1890–1938). Its main emphasis, following the influence of Ferdinand de **Saussure**, was on the analysis of language as a system of functionally related units.

prefixing language see **affixing language**

prescriptive Descriptive of any approach which attempts to lay down rules of correctness as to how language should be used, using such criteria as purity, logic, history, or literary excellence. Prescriptive grammars aim to preserve imagined standards by insisting on norms of usage and criticizing departures from these norms. A distinction is sometimes drawn between **prescriptive** and **proscriptive** rules, the latter being rules which forbid rather than command. Linguistics has been generally critical of the prescriptivist approach, emphasizing instead the importance of descriptively accurate studies of usage, and of the need to take into account sociolinguistic variation in explaining attitudes to language.

principles and parameters see **government and binding theory**

procedure see **discovery procedure; evaluation procedure**

production see **speech production**

productivity (1) The creative capacity of language users to produce and understand an indefinitely large number of sentences. It contrasts particularly with the **unproductive** communication systems of animals, and in this context is seen as one of the design features of human language. (2) The use made by a language of a specific feature or pattern. A pattern is productive if it is repeatedly used in language to produce further instances of the same type. An example of a productive pattern is the use of *-ed* to form the past tense of verbs in English; the use of vowel replacement to form the past tense (as in *take → took*) is an unproductive pattern.

proscriptive see **prescriptive**

proto- (1) A prefix used in **historical linguistics** to refer to a linguistic form or state of a language said to be the ancestor of attested forms or languages, as in the case of Proto-Indo-European or Proto-Germanic. (2) A prefix sometimes used in the study of child language **acquisition** for a pre-linguistic stage in the development of language, as when early **utterances** are said to be proto-sentences or part of a proto-conversation.

proto-conversation see **proto-**

proto-sentences see **proto-**

psycholinguistics A branch of linguistics which studies the correlation between linguistic behaviour and the mental processes and skills thought to underlie that behaviour, earlier called the **psychology of language**. The emphasis may be on the use of language as a means of elucidating psychological theories and processes (such as memory, attention, and learning), or on the effects of psychological constraints on the use of language (such as the role of memory in speech comprehension). It is the latter which has provided the main focus of interest in linguistics, where the subject is basically seen as the study of the mental processes underlying the planning, production, perception and comprehension of speech. The study of the **acquisition** of language by children is often distinguished as **developmental psycholinguistics**. (See also **applied linguistics**.)

psychology of language see **psycholinguistics**

purism A non-linguistic school of thought which sees language as needing preservation from the external processes which infiltrate it and thus make it change (as in the case of new pronunciations arising out of language or dialect contact, **loan words**, etc.). This view is opposed by linguists, who point to the inevitability of language change, as part of the process of social, cultural and psychological development.

quantitative linguistics A branch of linguistics which studies the frequency and distribution of linguistic units using statistical techniques. The subject's general aims are to establish principles governing the statistical regularities underlying the structure of language. Much of its work concerns the analysis of the linguistic features of particular texts (especially in literature), and the investigation of specific problems such as authorship identity.

realization The physical expression of an abstract linguistic unit. **Phonemes** are said to be 'realized' in phonic substance as phones; similarly, morphemes are realized as **morphs**. Any underlying form may be seen as having a corresponding realization at a less abstract level. Other terms for the same notion include **actualization** and **manifestation**, as well as the more general notions of **exponence** and representation.

reconstruction A method used in historical linguistics and comparative philology in which a hypothetical system of sounds or forms representing an earlier non-extant state of a language is established deductively from an analysis of the attested sounds and forms of extant texts. This process, called **comparative reconstruction**, is dependent on the existence of good written records or several known related languages. When these circumstances do not exist (as in many African languages), hypotheses about the historical development of the languages can still be made by analysing the structural regularities and irregularities of their contemporary states, and deducing underlying forms which might reflect earlier states. This process is called **internal reconstruction**.

redundant Descriptive of features whose presence is unnecessary in order to identify a linguistic unit or to make a linguistic contrast. For example, there is redundancy in the sentence *A dog barks*, because the expression of singularity is shown three times, by the indefinite article, the singular form of the noun, and the third person singular form of the verb. The notion is also relevant in **phonology**, where not all the features of sound may be needed in order to make a contrast in pronunciation. Voicing, muscular tension and aspiration combine to distinguish *pit* and *bit*, for example, but only one of these features is necessary to specify the contrast involved.

reference see **sense**

…e grammar see **grammar** (1)

referent In **semantics**, an entity (object, state of affairs, etc.) in the external world to which a linguistic expression refers; for example, the referent (or referential meaning) of the word *chair* is the object 'chair'. This extralinguistic notion of reference contrasts with the intralinguistic notion of **sense**, which arises from the meaning relations between lexical items and sentences.

referential meaning see **meaning; referent**

regular Descriptive of a linguistic form or pattern which conforms to the general rules of a language; in other words, it is predictable. For example, nouns such as *cat* and *dog* in English are regular, in that they make use of *-s* to form plurals; nouns such as *mouse* and *sheep* are **irregular**. In historical linguistics, regularity is a major explanatory principle, in that the subject aims to show systematic correspondences between languages and states of a language which can be formulated in a general way.

relational grammar A development of generative linguistics in the mid-1970s which takes as central the notion of grammatical relations (such as subject and object), rather than the formal categories (NP, VP, etc.) of previous approaches. A relational **network** is a formal representation of a sentence, showing the grammatical relations that elements of the sentence bear to each other, and the syntactic levels at which these relations hold.

relational network see **relational grammar**

relative universals see **universal**

relativity see **linguistic relativity**

representation see **exponence**; **realization**

revised extended standard theory (REST) The name given to the revised version of the **extended standard theory** of **generative grammar**, proposed by Noam **Chomsky** in the mid-1970s.

rule A formal statement of correspondence between linguistic elements or structures, especially used in **generative grammar**. Generative rules are predictive, expressing a hypothesis about the relationships between sentences which hold for a language as a whole, and which reflect the speaker's **competence**. The use of the term in linguistics contrasts with its use in traditional grammar, where it is a **prescriptive** recommendation about correct usage.

Sapir–Whorf Hypothesis see **linguistic relativity**

Saussure, Ferdinand de (1857–1913) Swiss linguist, widely recognized as the founder of modern linguistics, whose views are outlined in his posthumous *Cours de linguistique générale*, published in 1913. His conception of language as a system of mutually defining entities was a major influence on several later schools of linguistic thought. His theoretical insights include the distinction between **langue** and parole, **syntagmatic** and **paradigmatic**, **synchronic** and **diachronic**, and the nature of the linguistic sign. (See **semiotics**.)

scale-and-category grammar see **Halliday, M. A. K.**

script see **transcription**

63

segmental phonology see **phonology**

semantic component see **semantics**

semantic relations see **semantics**

semantics A branch of linguistics devoted to the study of meaning in language. In particular, the approach called structural semantics applies the principles of structural linguistics to the study of meaning through the notion of semantic relations between lexical items (such as synonymy and antonymy). In **generative grammar**, the semantic component is a major area of the organization of a grammar, which assigns a semantic representation to a sentence and analyses lexical items in terms of semantic features. In a wider context, philosophical semantics examines the relations between linguistic expressions and the phenomena in the world to which they refer, considering the conditions under which such expressions can be said to be true or false, and the factors which affect linguistic interpretation.

semiotics The study of signs and their use, focusing on the mechanisms and patterns of human **communication** (in all its modes – auditory, visual, tactile, etc.) and on the nature and acquisition of knowledge. Language is viewed as one type of sign system, along with such other systems as body gesture, clothing, dance, and the arts.

sense The meaning of a linguistic expression, such as a word or sentence. In linguistics, a distinction is usually drawn between sense and reference. Sense is the system of linguistic relationships (sense relations) which a lexical item contracts with other lexical items, such as the relationship of oppositeness which links *big* and *little*. Reference is an extralinguistic notion – the entities or states of affairs in the external world referred to by a linguistic expression. (See also **referent**.)

sense relations see **sense**

sentence The largest structural unit in terms of which the **grammar** of a language is organized. Most linguistic definitions emphasize the structural autonomy or independence of the sentence – that it is not part of a larger linguistic form. Formal classifications recognize such types as declarative, interrogative, and imperative; functional classifications recognize such types as statement, question, and command. Notional definitions (such as 'the sentence is the expression of a complete thought'), commonly employed in traditional language study, are avoided in modern linguistic approaches.

sentence structure see **structural**

sign language A system of gestures, made primarily with the hands, used to replace speech as a mode of **communication**. The most sophisticated sign languages are those which have developed naturally within deaf communities (such as American Sign Language). In addition, several kinds of sign language have been invented by educators to convey spoken language to the deaf, and other kinds have been developed by hearing people in special circumstances (such as for communication between members of a religious community vowed to silence).

significant see **contrast**

situational context see **context** (2)

situational meaning see **meaning**

sociolinguistics A branch of linguistics which studies all aspects of the relationship between language and society, especially with reference to such notions as race, ethnicity, class, sex, and social institutions. A distinction is often drawn between this subject and the **sociology of language** (or **sociological linguistics**) which tends to operate from the viewpoint of sociology, seeing language as an integral part of sociological theory. (See also **applied linguistics**.)

sociological linguistics see **sociolinguistics**

sociology of language see **sociolinguistics**

specialization A suggested defining property of human language, when this is contrasted with the properties of other **semiotic** systems, referring to the extent to which the use of a signal and the behaviour it evokes are directly linked. Animal communication is said to lack specialization, in that a signal triggers a behaviour. Language, by contrast, is highly specialized, as the behavioural consequences of using a linguistic signal are various and often unpredictable.

speech community A regionally or socially definable human group, which can be identified by the use of a shared language or language variety. A speech community might be extremely small, as encountered in many local dialects or tribal languages, or very large, as encountered in the use of English throughout the world.

speech perception The process of receiving and decoding speech input; it contrasts with **speech production**. The study involves the analysis of the way listeners extract phonetic and linguistic units from the acoustic cues present in the speech signal, and the study of the processes and mechanisms governing this ability. It must also take into account listeners' knowledge of the sound patterns of their language, which enables them to interpret what they hear.

speech production The process of planning and executing the act of speech; it contrasts with **speech perception**. The study includes the neuroanatomical and neurophysiological activities involved in speaking, as well as the construction and testing of models of the neural control system in the brain's organization of speech. Features of speech output (such as slips of the tongue) can be analysed as a means of inferring the properties of this system.

Sprachbund see **areal linguistics**

Sprachgefühl see **intuition, linguistic**

standard theory The model of **generative grammar** proposed by Noam **Chomsky** in *Aspects of the Theory of Syntax* in 1965. Despite many subsequent modifications, it is still often considered to be the main statement concerning the aims and form of a transformational grammar. Later developments included the **extended standard theory** and the **revised extended standard theory**.

starred form see **asterisked form**

statistical linguistics A branch of linguistics which studies the application of probabilistic techniques in linguistic theory and description. It includes the analysis of the frequency and distribution of linguistic units in texts, and the relationship between word types and tokens (i.e. the number of different words in a sample compared to the number of times each word appears).

string A linear sequence of elements of determinate length and constitution; for example, the sentence *the + dog + s + like + bone + s*. The term is especially used in **generative grammar**. A **substring** is any part of a string which is itself a string, such as *the + dog + s* in that example.

strong equivalence see **equivalence**

strongly adequate see **adequacy**

structural Descriptive of any approach to the analysis of language which pays explicit attention to the formal and functional patterns which constitute its organization. A structure, in this sense, is a network of interrelated units, the meaning of the parts being specifiable only with reference to the whole. The term is widely used with reference to particular sections of this total network, as in the discussion of sentence structure, phrase structure, syllable structure, and so on. Structuralism originally referred to an approach which emphasized the segmentation and classification of utterances, as proposed by Leonard **Bloomfield** and other **structural(ist)** linguists of the 1940s and 1950s. More generally, this term is used for the theory that any human institution (e.g., dance, eating, music) can be analysed in terms of an underlying network of formal and functional relationships.

structural ambiguity see **ambiguous**

structural(ist) linguists see **structural**

structural semantics see **semantics**

stylistics A branch of linguistics which studies the features of situationally distinctive uses (varieties or 'styles') of language, and tries to establish principles which account for the particular choices made by individuals and social groups in their use of language. In a narrower sense, it refers to the aesthetic use of language. When literature is the focus of attention, the subject is often called literary stylistics (or literary linguistics).

sub-component see **component**

substance The undifferentiated raw material out of which language is constructed — the sound waves of speech (phonic substance) and the marks on a surface which constitute writing (graphic substance). Substance is here opposed to **form**, the abstract pattern of relationships imposed on this substance by a language.

substantive universals see **universal**

substitution see **paradigmatic relations**

substring see **string**

suffixing language see **affixing language**

suprasegmental phonology see **phonology**

surface structure In **generative grammar**, the final stage in the syntactic representation of a sentence, which provides the input to the phonological component of the grammar. It thus most closely corresponds to the structure of the sentence which we articulate and hear. A contrast is implied with an underlying level of sentence structure, originally referred to as **deep structure**.

syllable structure see **structural**

synchronic linguistics One of the two main temporal dimensions of linguistic investigation introduced by Ferdinand de **Saussure**; it contrasted with **diachronic linguistics**. Languages are studied at a theoretical point in time: a 'state of the language' (**état de langue**) is described, disregarding whatever changes might be taking place. Most synchronic descriptions are of contemporary language states, but their importance as a preliminary to diachronic study has been stressed since Saussure.

syntactic component see **syntax**

syntactic structures see **syntax**

syntactics see **taxis**

syntagmatic relations The sequential relationships between the string of constituents in a construction; opposed to **paradigmatic relations**. For example, the relationships between the **phonemes** /p/, /i/, and /t/ in the word *pit* are syntagmatic, as are the relationships between the individual words in the phrase *the big car*. Syntagmatic relations can be established at all levels of analysis.

syntax The study of the rules governing the way words are combined to form sentences and other constructions in a language. In this use, syntax is opposed to **morphology**, the study of word structure. More generally, it is the study of the interrelationships between all elements of sentence structure (including **morphemes**), and of the rules governing the arrangement of sentences in sequences. In **generative grammar**, the syntactic component contains rules for the generation of syntactic structures.

synthetic language A type of language in which words typically contain more than one **morpheme**; opposed to an **analytic language**. Examples include Greek, Latin, and Turkish. Two types of synthetic language are usually recognized – **agglutinative** and **inflecting languages**, with polysynthetic languages sometimes additionally distinguished. (See also **typology**.)

system see **systemic grammar**

systemic grammar A grammatical theory developed by M. A. K. **Halliday** in the 1970s, in which the notion of paradigmatic relationship (or **system**) is made the central explanatory principle. Grammar is seen as a network of systems of relationships which account for all the semantically relevant choices in the language.

tacit knowledge see **intuition, linguistic**

tagmeme see **tagmemics**

tagmemics A system of analysis developed by Kenneth Pike (1912–), in which the relationship of phonology to phoneme and lexicon to morpheme is paralleled by the addition of grammar to tagmeme. A tagmeme is a functional slot within a construction frame, and a class of substitutable items that can fill this slot. The approach is widely used by the Summer Institute of Linguistics as part of the training of linguists.

taxis The systematic arrangement of units in linear sequence at any linguistic level. The commonest terms based on this notion are **phonotactics**, for the sequential arrangement of sounds; **morphotactics**, for the sequencing of **morphemes**; and **syntactics**, for the sequencing of higher grammatical units than the morpheme.

taxonomic linguistics An approach to linguistic analysis which is predominantly or exclusively concerned with procedures of segmentation and classification (**taxonomy**). In the history of linguistic thought, the notion contrasts with **generative grammar**, which stresses the role of underlying structure in linguistic analysis.

taxonomy see **taxonomic linguistics**

text A piece of naturally occurring spoken, written, or signed discourse identified for purposes of analysis. It is often a language unit with a definable communicative function (such as a conversation, a poster). The study of the defining properties or texts is carried on by **textlinguistics**. Several narrower definitions of the term are also found.

textlinguistics see **text**

textual competence see **competence**

theoretical grammar see **grammar** (2)

traditional grammar The set of attitudes, procedures and prescriptions characteristic of the prelinguistic era of language study, and especially of the European school grammars of the eighteenth and nineteenth centuries. The approach emphasized such matters as correctness, the purity of a language, literary excellence, the use of Latin models, and the priority of the written language over the spoken. It also passed on to contemporary linguistics several important grammatical notions, such as parts of speech and the techniques of clause analysis. (See **prescriptive**.)

transcript see **transcription**

transcription A method of writing down speech sounds in a systematic and consistent way; also called a **notation**, **script**, or **transcript**. In a **phonetic** transcription, sounds are symbolized on the basis of their articulatory and auditory identity, regardless of their function in a language. In a **phonemic** transcription, the only units to be symbolized are those which have a linguistic function. A phonetic transcription which is relatively detailed is a **narrow transcription**; one less detailed is a **broad transcription**.

transformation A formal linguistic operation which enables two levels of structural representation to be placed in correspondence. A **transformational rule** (T-rule) consists of a sequence of symbols which is rewritten as another sequence, according to certain conventions. A grammar which makes use of these rules is a **transformational grammar** (TG). In recent years, these grammars have been contrasted with non-transformational grammars, such as **generalized phrase-structure grammar**. (See also **generative grammar**.)

transformational grammar (TG) see **transformation**

transformational (T) rule see **transformation**

tree A two-dimensional diagram used in **generative grammar** as a convenient means of displaying the internal hierarchical structure of sentences generated by a set of rules. The 'root' of the tree is at the top, and from this point (or node) branches descend corresponding to the categories specified by the rules. The internal relationships of nodes within the tree are described using family tree terminology (mother, daughter, sister).

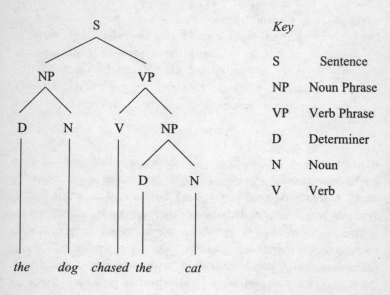

Fig. 3   A typical tree diagram, as used in one version of generative grammar

typological linguistics see **typology**

typology A branch of linguistics which studies the structural similarities between languages, regardless of their history; also called **typological linguistics**. The approach is essential in cases where languages lack a tradition of written records. Several types of language have been suggested, on this basis: see **affixing**; **agglutinative**; **analytic**; **inflectional**; **isolating**; **polysynthetic** and **synthetic language**.

ultimate constituents see **constituent**

underlying Descriptive of an abstract level of representation postulated to explain the patterns encountered in the empirical data of a language. The notion is central to **generative grammar**, where a stage of underlying structure is recognized in the derivation of a sentence.

ungrammatical see **grammaticality**

universal A property claimed to be characteristic of all languages – a defining property of language; also called a **linguistic universal**. **Universal grammar** aims to specify the possible forms of a human grammar, especially the restrictions on the form such grammars can take. **Absolute universals** are properties that all languages share, without exception. **Relative universals** are general tendencies in language, with principled exceptions. **Formal universals** are the necessary conditions that have to be imposed on the construction of grammars in order for them to be able to operate (e.g., types of rules). **Substantive universals** are the primitive elements in a grammar, required for the analysis of linguistic data, and classified into syntactic, phonological, and other types (e.g., the notions of noun phrase and sentence). Several other kinds of universal have been recognized.

universal grammar see **grammar**; **universal**

unmarked see **markedness**

unproductive see **productivity**

usage The speech and writing habits of a community, especially as presented descriptively with information about preferences for alternative linguistic forms. Linguists emphasize the importance of describing the facts of usage as a control on the claims made by grammars, and contrast this emphasis with the **prescriptive** attitudes of traditional grammars.

utterance A stretch of speech about which no assumptions have been made in terms of linguistic theory; usually opposed to the notion of **sentence**, which receives its definition from a theory of grammar. The notion is difficult to define, but utterances are typically preceded or followed by silence or a change of speaker.

variant see **allo-**

variety A system of linguistic expression whose use is governed by situational variables, such as regional, occupational or social class. The term is sometimes used more narrowly, referring to a single kind of situationally distinctive language, such as the variety of legal English or sports commentary.

vocalization An **utterance** viewed solely as sound. No reference is made to its linguistic structure, and in some contexts (such as 'infant vocalization') there may be no such structure.

weak equivalence see **equivalence**

weakly adequate see **adequacy**

well-formedness see **grammaticality**

Whorfian hypothesis see **linguistic relativity**

word see **lexeme**

word order see **order**

zero An abstract unit with no physical realization in the stream of speech; also called a **null element**. The term is commonly used for the absence of a **morpheme** in contexts where one would normally occur. Examples include the notion of zero article (when there is no definite or indefinite article before a noun in English) and zero morph (e.g., the absence of a plural marker in such nouns as *sheep*).

zero article see **zero**

zero morph see **zero**